UNDONE

HAUWA SALEH ABUBAKAR

Published by Akashic Books

ISBN: 978-1-63614-254-8

Printed in China
First printing

EU Authorized Representative details:
Easy Access System Europe
Mustamäe tee 50, 10621 Tallinn, Estonia
gpsr.request@easproject.com

Akashic Books
Instagram, X, Facebook: AkashicBooks
info@akashicbooks.com
www.akashicbooks.com

African Poetry Book Fund
Brown University
10 Prospect Street
Box A
Providence, RI 02912

To Dr Saleh Abubakar—who before he became my father, found himself in the lines of poetry:

Cry not black woman,
for having drank your milk
we drink too of life
and so must die.

—Dr. Saleh Abubakar, "To My Mother"

TABLE OF CONTENTS

PREFACE

by Safia Elhillo

A tender and clear-eyed meditation on bereavement and longing, *Undone* by Nigerian poet and journalist Hauwa Saleh Abubakar is a portrait of a loved one's passing. Reading these poems, I think back to that old adage that death is only sad for those left behind. The grief here is not a violent nor a vengeful presence, simply a force of nature to be contended with, observed, and eventually integrated.

With intimacy and care, Abubakar's speaker opens and dissects her own and her family's grief over the passing of her father. Her observations are precise, detailed, and specific. The grief is tangible as a body:

> Sometimes my mother's grief wraps itself
> around her like a snake,
> pulling her down with its weight.
> My grief hangs like a cloud above my head.
>
> ("How to Rest a Grieving Body")

In these poems, the personification of grief animates it, imbues it with flesh, blood, and spirit—breathes, ironically, life into it. And through this anthropomorphism, grief becomes a new member of the mourning family. It demands to be reckoned with, cared for, even loved: "I took my grief to a beach today . . . We dipped our legs in the water . . . We stared at the resting evening sun . . . Then my grief held my hand" ("At the Beach"). Grief is a point of comparison and connection between mother and daughter, and is worn by the speaker's brother as a skin—this grief that is both the presence and absence of the lost father, the lost husband.

In addition to the recurring anthropomorphizing gesture, these poems engage intimately with ritual. The speaker finds agency in the face of devastating loss through the construction of personal rituals, ranging from taking her grief to the beach, to simply making tea:

> But I can tell you
> the night my father passed,
> right after I tried to pull some of the pain
> out of my eyes,
> I still gathered enough strength
> to grab a tea bag,
> drop it into a cup
> and watch it sink and bleed into the water.
>
> ("Mouthful")

The healing and transformative power of water is omnipresent throughout the collection, encountered in tears, tea, or the vastness of the sea. Each image of water in these poems gestures toward the potential to cleanse away grief, guilt, and longing, and make room for what comes after.

This powerful ritual work, this reckoning with grief, is not uncomplicated. In "I Did It Again," the poet examines the ways the bereaved person can also be profoundly selfish, casting their pain onto their perception of other people's experiences, even when unwarranted: "I did not even remember her face. / Yet I say I am sorry like I have held her in my belly for nine months." This is generous, delicate work: to hold space and love for the self in mourning, while simultaneously holding to account the ways in which grief can self-center, can reorient our world's orbit around this locus of pain and loss.

In these poems, Abubakar's language is spare and direct, stripped bare by pain, both beautiful and unadorned. The details, the clarity of the looking, sear themselves into my memory: the father's white kaftan, worn by her brother; the figurine sitting on the mantle, barely salvaged from the fire. This collection is constructed with such care, such closeness of attention. In the final poem, "I Completed the Pot," Abubakar's speaker articulates the hope that the pot she is making will "absorb some of my sadness / and embed it into something beautiful." This collection is proof of that aspiration to "*make something out of this pain*" ("I Completed the Pot").

And yet, as in life, the journey of these poems does not come neatly to an end, but continues to echo out, to haunt. The collection draws to a close on a hopeful note, while simultaneously leaving an opening for the work of healing to continue, to bloom alongside the grief. And Abubakar's speaker grows alongside both the grief and the healing, learning the lifelong work of carrying them.

FORGIVE ME FATHER, FOR I HAVE SINNED

Cancer had been at the edge of my tongue
ever since I came
undone in my cousin's bathroom.
Weeks after that I found myself falling deeper into the hole
but I never showed anyone I knew
what you were so desperately trying to hide.
I could only think of all the days I had been sick
and your soft knocks would come at the door
asking if I was okay because you didn't see me that day.
I wondered how long you held the word in your mouth,
ran it over your tongue and let it fester.
I am sorry that at first, I couldn't see the pain
you were trying so desperately to hide.

Even when you laid there helpless on the bed
my mind couldn't stop thinking about how difficult it was for us
to be going through this.
I prayed for relief but a part of me didn't want to deal
with this loss,
a part of me still wanted you to breathe even longer,
even on the nights your screams tore through the walls
and left their marks in us.

Can you remember the day you tried to peel a banana,
how it found its way under your fingernails,
sticking to your skin?
But even when you drifted off to sleep and I cleaned it off your hands
I still wanted you here.

When my cousin called me to offer her condolences,
pausing my song in its track,
arresting the breath in my lungs,
my first thought was how free you can be now of this pain.
But I wasn't strong enough to let you go.
I said I was glad,
but I still broke down near the body
that looked so much better than it did
when you were alive.

I didn't want to call it just the body,
even though I knew you weren't there anymore.

Forgive me father,
for I have sinned.

I DREAMED OF MY FATHER TODAY . . .

This was the first time he'd visited me since he left.
He was sitting healthy on a bed,
but I found myself walking on the opposite side
and no matter how fast I walked,
I still couldn't reach him.

Even in a dream,
it seems like some things are unreachable.
Even in a dream,
it seems like some longings cannot
be fed.

I am worried I will dream of my father again,
and no matter how fast I walk
I still will never reach him.

HOW TO REST A GRIEVING BODY

Sometimes my mother's grief wraps itself
around her like a snake,
pulling her down with its weight.
My grief hangs like a cloud above my head.
My mother and I
hold our griefs against the light.

When my mother and I compare our grief notes
We find the same truth:
We are missing him today.

To comfort a grieving body, you must
rest it gently against another grieving body
and let them sway to the beat of memories.

AT THE BEACH

I took my grief to a beach today,
it folded into something that could fit in my purse.
We dipped our legs in the water,
and some of the pain melted into the sea.

We stared at the resting evening sun
and talked about the lives we once had.

Then my grief held my hand
and together we wrote my name in the sand.
We chose a place where the water
could not swallow it.

We stared at it for a while,
and then I packed my bag
and went back home.

MOUTHFUL

I cannot tell you
just how much I love tea,
how it always manages to bring me home to myself
no matter how much I am drowning at sea.
But I can tell you
the night my father passed,
right after I tried to pull some of the pain
out of my eyes,
I still gathered enough strength
to grab a tea bag,
drop it into a cup
and watch it sink and bleed into the water.

Then I sat down
with everything I was feeling
and not feeling,
with everything I wish I had said
and everything I couldn't take back,
with the tears and the heaviness
hanging in the air around me,
threatening to crush my lungs,
and I sipped my tea.

CURES WORK AFTER DEATH TOO

They said they found a cure for cancer
less than three weeks after you left.
But the joy flowed like a stream through my veins
because no one would have to tear cotton wool apart
to clean their loved one's blood.
No one would have to sit through their loved one's screams
unsure of what to do.
No one would have to watch their loved one
tied to a bed
with tubes attached,
taking pint after pint of blood.
And when we walk for cancer
we will only have to worry about those who have passed.
We will talk about how chemotherapy was a painful,
harrowing thing of the past.
We will have fewer blood donations,
and when we gather around the fire,
we will speak not only of loss, but of hope.
We will cry because you are gone,
but we will also laugh because
fewer will have to walk this path now.

WHITE IS THE SHADE OF SURRENDER

My brother wore my father's white kaftan today.
It fit so perfectly that for a moment
I could picture exactly what he once looked like in it;
the way it sat on his body
just enough to cover his whole being
without smothering him,
the way his funeral shroud did.
And for a moment
everything could be true
in another universe.
He was well enough to visit friends before he would leave.
No medications left him delirious on the bed,
no heart-wrenching screams escaped his lips.
He could laugh and crack jokes,
and I got to say goodbye.
In another world,
he wore this white kaftan on his last day.
Even the pain knew better than to stay close.

WOULD YOU STILL LOVE ME IF I WAS A ZOMBIE?

Some days
I worry I am too heavy for my lover to carry.
These are the moments I fold into myself,
and when I get the strength, I ask,
Would you still love me if I was a zombie?
To which my very logical lover says,
But you wouldn't be you anymore.
On those days
I laugh and say
something like,
What happened to hiding me in the
basement and finding a cure?
But we both know
I was a zombie today,
and my lover didn't go running to the door.
If tomorrow I become a zombie again
I will ask differently:
Do you love me today?
And the answer will always be,
Yes.
Even now that I can no longer call
my lover, *my lover*
I throw the question into the void,
and the echo answers back,
Yes.

REVOLUTION

I am terrified of being held for too long.
I worry that if someone's fingertips linger
for too long on my skin
I will unravel from the core.
All my edges will fall off
like the dried leaves off a tree in harmattan.
I worry I will be lost to the wind,
that it will gather me in its arms
and take me far above the clouds,
and I will lose my ground.

When someone's tenderness touches the soft,
fragile surface of my skin,
I feel it start at the bottom of my stomach,
a small revolution
threatening to tear me apart.
But I want to be whole.
Let me be whole.
Let me keep this ground.

THINGS LEFT BEHIND

I fear nothing
more than leaving behind my things unorganized—
when I die, I can't bear the thought of my loved ones sifting through
piles of clothes, jeans, mixed in with gowns and old socks. That
is why, every time I leave the house, I make sure to keep everything
in its place just in case I die on the road.

I organize my left-behind undies in their drawer, keep the socks separate
from the pants, the pants from the bras. Keep the clothes neatly arranged, make sure
the books are all in place, organized on the lower layer of the wardrobe, till
one day I make the decision to build them a shelf of their own.

And when I am gone, my loved ones won't have to lose themselves
in my mess. If one day I die on the road, no one will have to sit through
the pain of sorting out the things I should have sorted out while my heart was
still beating
in my chest. And maybe at that moment they would say,
that girl, that girl had it all figured out.

Look at all the time we've been saved to grieve. Look at all this care urging us
to remember, to remember that there was a girl who lived here, who remembered
to keep all her things in her drawer, who remembered there is so much to sort
out already
and didn't add anything to the pile.

I DID IT AGAIN

I forced my way into your house of grief,
studied the lines on your face and attempted
to trace them onto mine.
I am a shameless thief, feeling entitled to this grief
that does not belong to me.
I am sorry for your loss, I said,
as if my words could find a way to bring back all it was.
The woman close to me held your hands
and your body crumbled under the weight of your tears.
I turned my face away,
my heart tumbling into my stomach.
I did not even remember her face.
Yet I say I am sorry like I have held her in my belly for nine months,
like I remember what she smelled like when she was three,
like her name weighs down my tongue when I try to say it.
I did it again.
I stole a grief that does not belong to me.
Said sorry to you over and over again.
But I do not know
if I am sorry for pretending to know your pain,
pretending that I know
just how heavy this weight can be.

WHAT I LEARNED FROM THE FIRE

i. Abandon what you can and run.

ii. You can't salvage everything from the burning flames, but you can salvage what you can of your body, your mother's favorite pillow, your father's favorite mug, and the figurine that had been sitting on the mantle for as long as you could remember.

iii. The fire leaves its mark for years to come.

iv. The flames glow like the sun. The light is now yours to use.

v. Scrape the ashes from the floor—build a castle, build a palace, build a shrine, build everything you can to make sure this body never burns again.

HOW TO PRACTICE FORGETTING

i.
You breathe through your nose
and ignore all the dust it drags along.

ii.
You cut your memories into little pieces,
small enough to slip through your fingers,
even before you are brave enough to let them go.

iii.
You allow them to haunt your body.
Let the barricades down,
don't try to hide the cobwebs,
no, not yet.
Let every ghost have their turn
so that when they try to come back,
they will remember there is nothing left for them here.

iv.
Start practicing how to throw away scents
and ignore the shell of a ghost knocking on your door.

v.
When you practice forgetting
you do not fight with memories.
You give them a space to replay themselves over and over again
until they fade away from remembering.

I COMPLETED THE POT

I was working on when you died.
Maybe I thought it would absorb some of my sadness
and embed it into something beautiful,
and when tomorrow came,
I could look at the green, red, and blue patterns and say
I was able to make something out of this pain.
Maybe I thought
if I placed it on a shelf,
it would be a wonderful reminder of all the times
I had been forced to be strong.

I completed the pot today,
but your bed was still empty when I laid down on it,
and the sadness still sat heavy on my chest.

But, my god,
have you seen that pot?
What a beautiful way to forget I was absent when you left.
What a beautiful way to forget how you had to
lock yourself inside, in an attempt to escape the pain,
but it still found ways of slipping out of your body.

Maybe there is healing here,
maybe this too
is healing.

ACKNOWLEDGMENTS

"I Dreamed Of My Father Today," *Ake Review*, 2022
"White Is The Shade Of Surrender," *Lolwe*, issue 8
"Revolution," *Ake Review*, 2022
"Things Left Behind," *Ake Review*, 2020